CAN YOU SEE ME?

Images of Atlanta's Homeless

Marmac Publishing Company, Inc.

SPECIAL THANKS

We would like to give special thanks to Chrys Graham and Anita Beaty, whose inspiration, ideas and commitment made this book possible; Keith Graham, for the Herculean task of interviewing and coaxing words out of 33 photographers; Regina Swim, for persistence, patience and striving for perfection in the production of this book; Nancy Roquemore, for making sure all the i's were dotted and all the t's were crossed. Marge McDonald and Kathy Shaw with Marmac Publishing, for their expertise and faith; Gail Goodwin, owner of The Highland Gallery, for framing the photographs for exhibition, and Suzanne Miller with Meisel for her last minute enthusiasm and assistance.

"Can You See Me?" was produced with grants from the City of Atlanta, The Atlanta Journal and The Atlanta Constitution, and the Atlanta Task Force for the Homeless.

CREDITS

Editor
Billy Howard

Assistant Editor
Louie Favorite

Introduction
Lee Walburn
Columnist for The Atlanta Journal
and The Atlanta Constitution

Designer
Stacy Sweat

Special Contributors
Kathleen Harbin
Alan Weiner
William Berry

Printed by Hunter Publishing Company
Winston-Salem, N.C.

First Edition, 1986

Requests for permission to reproduce material from this work should be sent to Marmac Publishing Company, 3423 Piedmont Rd., Suite 212, Atlanta Ga., 30305. 404/231-1131.

ISBN - 0939944-48-0

CONTENTS

Proceeds from this book will
go to the Homeless Task Force
and the Atlanta Community Food Bank.

PREFACE

Hope.

That one word, that feeling, more than any other, sums up the purpose of "Can You See Me?"

Hope that as photographers we can make a difference. That our images can individually and collectively motivate the viewer and initiate change. Hope that by looking into the faces of the homeless we see their dignity as well as their despair.

Hope, above all, that Atlanta's homeless find hope.

Hope that there is a home for each of us.

— Billy Howard

DEDICATION

This book is dedicated to the memory of Tom Vaughn, homeless Atlantan, who died under a bridge in an affluent Atlanta neighborhood two days after being photographed. And to Al Smith, "Gypsy," who left the streets and became assistant director of Samaritan House Shelter. Gypsy's life was a testament that there is hope for the homeless. He died October 17, 1986.

INTRODUCTION

He was standing as still as a wooden Indian and his face was lined like a giant piece of walnut that had cracked open from too much exposure to rain and wind and sun. Suddenly he began to weave and seemed to melt.

He fell into the street right in front of me. He was lying there, shaking, and it was obvious he would be struck by a passing car if we did not move him. Another man and I dragged him back onto the sidewalk and I asked a passerby to go inside a nearby building to call for help. The security guard inside the lobby said the sidewalk was not in his jurisdiction.

Finally an ambulance was called. I asked if the man needed anything. His eyes had the distant stare of someone gazing hard into some vaguely remembered past. He said, "I want to go home."

There was no home, except dormant thoughts that sometimes caught on the wind and blew like scrap paper down the back alleys of his mind. Merely in the struggle to remember, he was as close to a home as he had been in a long time.

He was one of Atlanta's 3,000-6,000 homeless men and women.

City government proposes laws to keep them out of sight of sensitive tourists and the affluent suburbanites, lest those with money in their pockets get the impression that downtown is not perfect. The homeless are called "a perception problem." The proposals answer everything except where they are to go.

There is always supposed to be somewhere to go home to. Street people are for New York and Chicago and Newark — cities of great transitions and rootlessness. Southerners are *supposed to have some place to go home to.*

Stripped of the essence of their heritage, Atlanta street people just wander. Some manage to spend their days in shelters. Others materialize on the avenues like scruffy apparitions. A woman layered in ragged clothing pushes at the refuse of an alley trash can with slow patient prospecting. A man in a found trucker's cap tries to keep his hand still long enough to light the inch-long butt of a cigarette.

A businessman hurrying to an early meeting passes without really being aware of them. At times they must feel invisible. Not because they are not there, but because no one wants to see.

There is an undeniable weakness of character about the street people. Most drink too much, eat too little and cannot care for themselves in a conventional manner. But in ways, they are stronger than most of us. Like ironweed they live in the toughest of circumstances and they hang on when hanging on would seem foolish to the supposedly rational among us. There is a primeval instinct to live that supercedes a modern tendency to give in.

What is it that keeps the human spirit alive in a body that is always too hot or too cold, a stomach that is always too hungry, a hand that clutches a bottle always too empty?

What happens when they long for sex and reach to touch skin that is like peeling paint and smell the breath of decaying food and twice-tasted whiskey?

Do they fantasize about perfume and fancy colognes?

Or do they just want to go home?

— Lee Walburn

THE
PHOTOGRAPHS

I felt really sorry for her. She was standing out on the sidewalk at the Fox. She was really sad, and she kept asking people for money. I bought a cupcake at a bakery for her, but she said, 'I don't want that cupcake. You're going to poison me.' I left it there, and I know she took it.

— *Margaret Barrett*

It was shot at St. Luke's at the soup kitchen on an assignment. It was nice to go over there because I have been a member of St. Luke's for a number of years. I went over expecting to see something very pathetic. Instead, what I found was a lot of dignity — for their place in the larger community despite what their present situation was. There was just a sense of 'There but for the grace of God, you might be in my place.' I was happy to be able to contribute this picture because there's something in the face of this guy. It's not pride in being poor but a sense of himself. I think it has to do with the attitude of the St. Luke's volunteers. There is a lot of interchange between the volunteers and the people who come to the soup kitchen.

— *Cheryl Bray*

People when they think of the homeless think of street winos, and that isn't really it. I think like 40 percent of the homeless are women. You don't think of children as homeless but there are a lot of them out there. To have children and have to sleep somewhere and get up by 6 a.m. and get them together and have to go out on the streets, that's some doing. I think it's really a sad thing in America in a day that we have a president who looks around and says he sees no signs of poverty.

— *Laura Sikes*

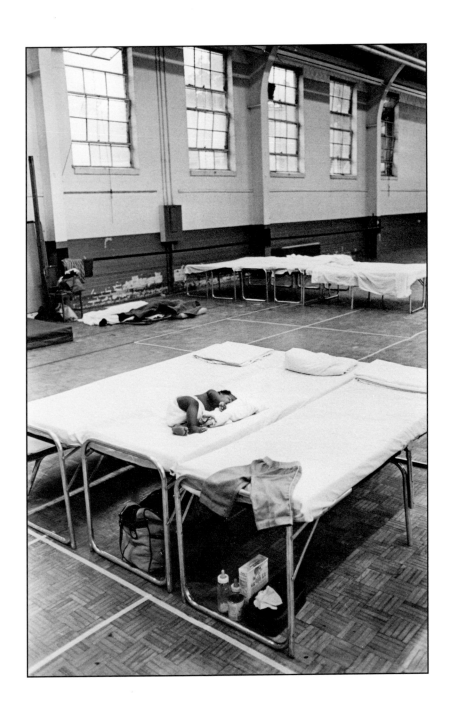

I took the photograph in the Union Mission, and when I went in people were outside the building drinking Heaven Hill bourbon. They offered me some, but I passed on that. This was the first time I'd approached homeless people or people on that side of the fringe. I was impressed with how generous they were. It seemed like they wanted me to accept them. Most people look out of the periphery of their eyes at the homeless because that's what they want to do. Photography is a way of looking straight in the eyes and seeing the dignity that these people have.

— *Billy Howard*

There was just this one old man who sat in the corner and seemed very upset. I noticed his hands shaking. He didn't know what to do with them. He seemed very lost. It sort of summed up for me his hopelessness.

— *Neil McGahee*

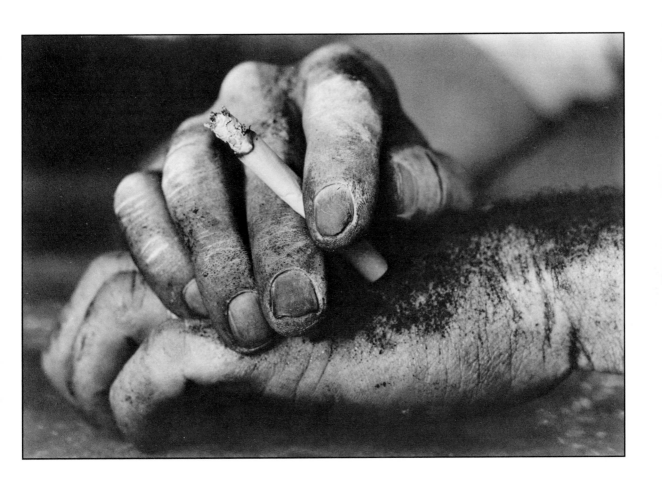

I was driving down a rural Georgia road close to Atlanta and saw this lady sitting by the side of the road hitchhiking with all her belongings. She was reading the Bible. She said she was a preacher. She was going nowhere, and, if she did get a ride, it didn't matter where.

— *Rich Addicks*

He didn't have much to say. He was just in Atlanta until the peach crop got better and then he was going to go pick fruit. He wasn't a hard-luck story like the rest of 'em. He was but he wasn't feeling sorry for himself. He was just doing the best he could do. He was trying to find work while he was here.

— Joey Ivansco

I'd heard that not only were there homeless people but people who had relationships with each other who were both homeless. This couple was originally from New England but had come to Atlanta. I tried to show that there was this relationship that was one of affection from both to both. It was kind of a special event for them — a family portrait.

— Alan David

When I added my presence to the scene there, it sort of made the surrounding people pay more attention. People were going out of their way to ignore that whole scene. Just the fact that I was there made them listen and watch more closely.

— *Tom S. England*

What surprised me most about
Frank was, when I found him out just
sleeping in this area with trees and
kudzu, there were books all around. I
found the guy was really well read. He
had been to college and worked at a lot
of jobs, but he's had some bad breaks
in his life. He was not someone to be
afraid of. He was just a real kind,
gentle person. One of his favorite
authors is John Updike, and one of
the books he was reading was about the
early American Federalists. Now he
makes some money as a powder
monkey. He sets dynamite kegs for
construction companies.

— *Wayne Martin*

Homelessness in downtown Atlanta creates countless confrontations between those with the 'least' in our culture and those with the most. Usually, the least lose the battle for space, dignity and recognition.

— Rob Johnson

This guy walks up to me and to my astonishment says, 'You're working on a book, aren't you?' We just started chatting, and I asked him if he'd give me a tour of all the old wino haunts. He's walking up some of those steps along Ponce de Leon where there used to be buildings but there are no buildings anymore. Steps leading to nowhere. I don't want to get philosophical about this. I don't know whether the man could quit drinking and lead another way of life. I don't know whether he's a victim of society or not.

— *George Mitchell*

This woman had lost her job. And she'd lost her boyfriend. And she didn't have any money. She didn't have any where else to stay.

— *Martha Leonard*

It was one of those things where I just set up a backdrop (on Ponce de Leon) and let people wander by and see what happened. He really was a ham and wanted to have his picture made. It was like his own stage presentation. The thing that really struck me was when I found out only about a week ago that he had died. You always think you're going to run into people like that again, but it really made me realize that life on the street is one of those things that obviously is real fleeting.

— *Alan Weiner*

This guy had just gotten beaten up. What was going through my mind is that street people are not a victim of society as much as they're a victim of their own conditioning. In a nutshell, what was on my mind is human conditioning from birth. 'A child who lives with criticism learns to condemn.... A child who lives with praise learns to be appreciative.'

— *Chris Savas*

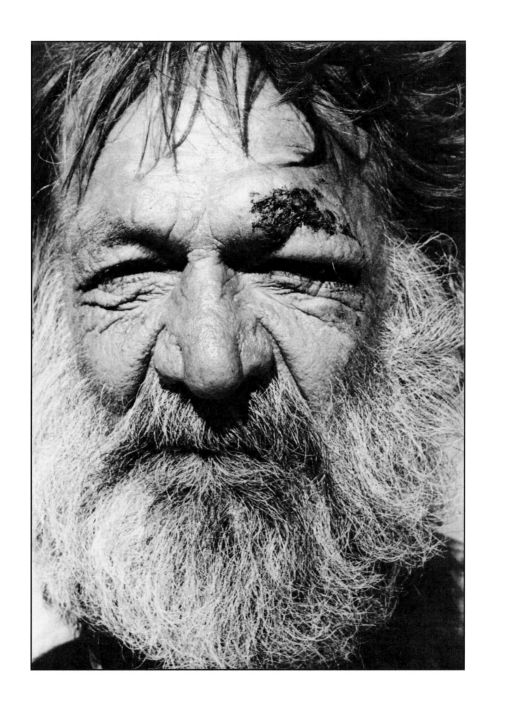

This little girl's name is Katrina Scott. She's nine years old. She's in a very delicate situation right now but she seemed very accepting and resilient. She told me that her mama is a chef at the YWCA. That's where they stay at night. She kept talking about food an awful lot. Food and schedule seemed to be the things that came to mind. 'Sometimes we go up to the pancake house and eat,' she said. 'When mama runs out of money we don't.'

— *Ann Youngling*

I was in the emergency room at Grady Hospital like all times of the day. I got to see all kinds of people coming through there. This was at 1 a.m. Most of the street people come in early in the morning. Those two people were comforting each other. People like that do try to help each other. They have their own codes of ethics.

— *Stephen Cord*

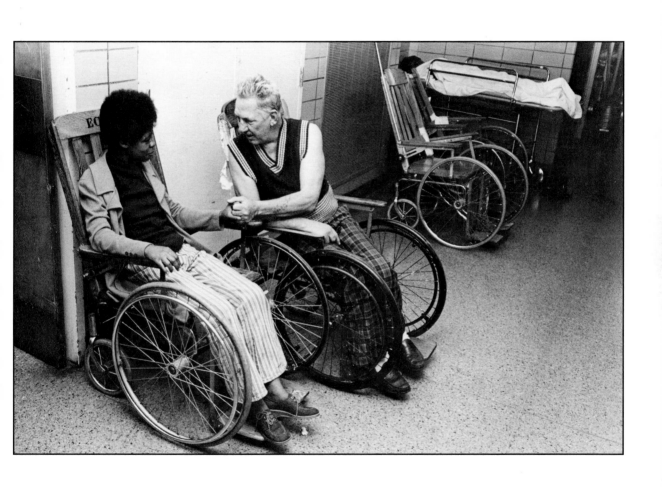

The man in the picture had lived there at least a dozen years, and they had just given him his eviction notice. The man was no derelict or wino. He quoted William Faulkner, and he had a lot of classic literature on his shelves. He didn't know what he was going to do. He was just bemoaning the fact that he was leaving.

— *Dennis Darling*

I saw Connie the day before and asked if I could photograph her. She said no, wait till the next day when she could put on some makeup and dress up. She said, 'Come see me tomorrow, and I'll be a different person. You won't even recognize me.' She wanted the pictures for her boyfriend. It seemed to mean a great deal to her.

— *Ann States*

Each time I've been to the Union
Mission the people have been real nice.
They are all friendly. They seem proud
and not embarrassed. I just have real
strong images of the people I've met.

— *Kelly Wilkinson*

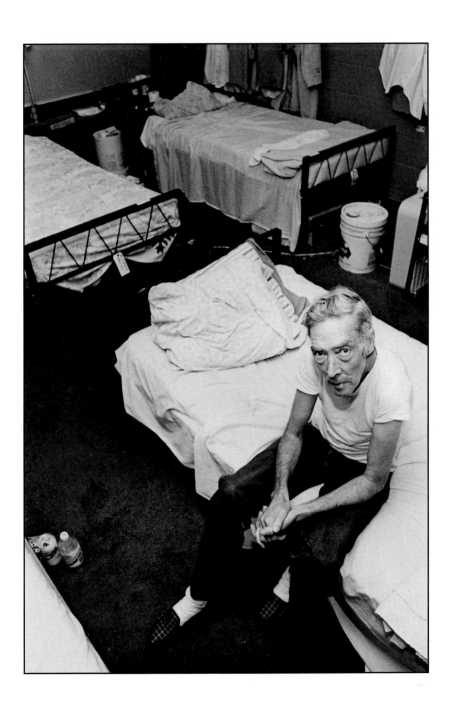

He took better care of his bottle than he did himself. He was just hugging the gutter and the bottle was upright. And people were just driving by. People don't care. That's the kind of thing that disturbs me.

— *John Rossino*

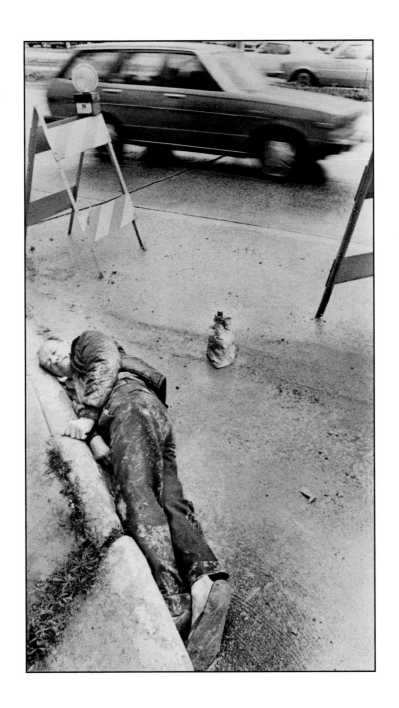

When the last cars have gone from the parking garage, James Hall and a dozen or more other street people take over, bringing in their bags, cardboard boxes and newspapers. 'You're scared to go to sleep 'cause you don't know who's going to sneak up on you,' Hall said. 'It's a half sleep. That's why you see so many people sleeping during the day.' Hall is an articulate, soft-spoken man. He was working on a construction job when the whole crew got fired. 'I lost my apartment because I couldn't pay the rent. I put my furniture in storage, but I lost that because I couldn't pay the storage,' he said.

— *Barbara McKenzie*

For the homeless, the greatest deprivations are not food and shelter but the loss of human warmth and sexual identity.

— *Gerald Jones*

He was sitting there in the stairwell. He didn't ask me for anything, but when he saw me pointing the camera at him he propped up a little, just showing that he had some dignity. I've taken a lot of pictures in boardrooms of corporate presidents, and I see the same thing there. There is a proud look in his eyes.

— W.A. Bridges, Jr.

He was lighting a cigarette that he'd rolled himself. I talked to him for a while. I felt like the things he told me he'd told to a hundred people before. He has his life together in terms of that kind of lifestyle.

— *Kathryn Kolb*

For a person like me and probably you, if we need food we go to the store or the restaurant or we just open up a refrigerator at home. For homeless people, there isn't that resource. If they have money, every penny counts. That's one of the things so important about a community soup kitchen. This is one meal for the entire day. Think how drained you feel at the end of a day even when you've had three square meals.

— Mark Sandlin

I call her Barbara of Auburn Avenue. Barbara is a sister who has survived. She has a pure soul, and she is really beautiful. I got to really know her, and we have an affinity because of her soul. She just hangs out. She's proud, very proud.

— *Dan Danner*

I have had a great deal of empathy for the homeless. It must be one of the most horrible things to be on the street and suffer all those losses. Just think about it. One day I walked by, and I saw this picture, and the image I had immediately is, one is a leader and the rest are disciples. They posed themselves. This one just exemplifies leadership on the streets. Obviously, they're out to find a drink or some solace somewhere.

— *Oraien Catledge*

I asked her to show me around the shelter. We walked out a door into a hall, and she said, 'This is my bedroom.' We're standing out in the hall. That's all it was. Just an old mattress thrown down there.

— Louie Favorite

A lot of homeless people sort of live out in the kudzu. This one mound of kudzu looks like a cave, and I've seen homeless people coming in and out of it a lot.

— *John McWilliams*

I can remember feeling real uncomfortable about being there. I can remember feeling sad — and scared. Yeah, I was scared. That was my very first experience with the homeless. Since then, I've gotten to know more of them, and there's not that feeling of a big difference between me and them anymore. A lot of them are very angry, and I can appreciate their anger.

— *Marilyn Futterman*

This little girl just had this flower.
She was holding on to that and eating
her macaroni soup or whatever. And she
just had this look about her. She knew
she was in a place where people didn't
have enough money to buy food. And
that was bothering her. It was just start-
ing to sink in. It really bothered me, too.
I've got a little boy who's 2.

— Rob Nelson

The first time I went down there — under a bridge at Montgomery Ferry next to the Ansley Golf Club — was on a Thursday. There was a Tom, Lloyd and Norton. Just hanging out. They said they'd just stopped by but you could tell they'd been there for a while. That Sunday I went back and Norton was sleeping so I woke him up. I mistakenly called him Tom, and he said, 'Tom's dead. He died Saturday.' I asked him what happened, but he said he didn't know. I called the Fulton County medical examiner's office, and they told me his name was Tom Vaughn and that he had died of drinking Lysol. They tried to find next of kin but he had no known address and no one claimed him. . .

. . . He was buried in a pauper's grave.
Even though they knew his name,
there's no marker.

— *William Berry*

The truth is: there are no
such things as Real homes
On this earth.
The dens we call pleasure domes
Will blend with the sand
and be placed in the shaker
Of time and scattered
across the universe.
We must meet and come to terms
with the Maker
Or else perpetually struggle
with that which is the reverse
Of life of love of bless:
stark homelessness.

By Billy Hands Robinson

Billy Hands Robinson is a poet from the Empty Spoon,
a collective of homeless writers.

Metro-Atlanta Homeless Shelter List

This list was prepared by the staff of The Task Force for the Homeless and includes all known shelters. Note that many of those listed under "night shelters" remain open 24 hours. For further information, call the Task Force office at 872-3603 or write The Task Force for the Homeless, 970 Jefferson St. N.W., Atlanta, GA. 30318.

Night Shelters

All Saints Episcopal Church, 645 Spring St. N.W., Atlanta, GA. 30308. 875-3924. Open Dec. 1-March 31. 50 men.

Atlanta Recovery Center, 169 Trinity Ave. S.W., Atlanta, GA. 30303. 577-3352. Open year round. 150 men.

Atlanta Union Mission — Men's Division, 200 Doane St. S.E., Atlanta, GA. 30315. 659-1708, 659-1709. Open year round. 275 men.

Atlanta Union Mission — Women's Division, 921 Howell Mill Road N.W., Atlanta, GA. 30318. 874-0891. Open year round. 93 women.

Belvedere Seventh Day Adventist, 3567 Covington Highway, Decatur, GA. 30030. 299-1359. Open October-March. 20 men.

Born Again Christian Center, 479 Marietta St. N.W., Atlanta, GA. 30303. 586-0449. Open year round. 10 men.

Calvary Baptist Church, 4234 Hendrix Drive, Forest Park, GA. 30050. 366-8753. Open Nov. 1-March 31. 50 men, women and children.

Cathedral of Faith, 1137 Avon Ave. S.W., Atlanta, GA. 30310. 752-8960. Open Nov. 1-March 31. 30 men.

Cathedral of Saint Philip, 2744 Peachtree Road N.W., Atlanta, GA. 30305. 261-3810. Open Nov. 16-March 15. 15 women and children.

Central Presbyterian Church, 201 Washington St. S.W., Atlanta, GA. 30303. 659-0274. Open Nov. 15-April 1. 75 men, women and children.

Clayton County Emergency, 173 Lee St., Jonesboro, GA. 30237. 361-0893. Open Nov. 1-March 31. 50 men, women and children.

Clifton Presbyterian Church Night Hospitality, 369 Connecticut Ave. N.E., Atlanta, GA. 30307. 373-3253. Open year round. 30 men.

Council on Battered Women, P.O. Box 54727, Atlanta, GA. 30308. 873-1766. Open year round. 11 women, 22 children.

Druid Hills Presbyterian Church, 1026 Ponce de Leon Ave. N.E., Atlanta, GA. 30306. 875-7591. Open Oct. 29-April 30. 30 men.

Elizabeth United Methodist "MUST" Ministries, 907 Church St., Marietta, GA. 30060. 427-9862. Open year round. 3 families.

First Presbyterian Church, 1328 Peachtree St. N.E., Atlanta, GA. 30357. 892-8463. (Shelter 874-1977.) Open year round. 12 women.

Fresh Start Ministries, 18 William H. Borders Drive S.E., Atlanta, GA. 30312. 688-8949. Open year round. 40 men.

Golden Harvest Mission, 202 Milton Ave. S.E., Atlanta, GA. 30315. 622-3409. Open year round. 200 men, women and children; 100 men overflow from city shelter.

Gospel Light Rescue Mission, 352 Peachtree St. N.E., Atlanta, GA. 30308. 577-3409. Open year round.

Harvest House, 475 Hill St. S.E., Atlanta, GA. 30312. 577-1538. Open year round. 20 men, women and children.

Help House, 830 Boulevard S.E., Atlanta, GA. 30312. 627-8447. Open year round. 10 families, 4 single men, 8 single women.

Holy Trinity Episcopal Church, 515 East Ponce de Leon Ave., Decatur, GA. 30030. 377-2622, 377-5365. Open Nov. 1-March 31. 15 women and children.

Mount Pleasant Baptist Church, 17 Meldon Ave. S.E., Atlanta, GA. 30315. 688-6680. Open Nov. 1-April 1. 25 men.

New Birth Christian Ministries, Inc., 485 Edgewood Ave. S.E., Atlanta, GA. 30312. 696-4964. Open year round. 3 families.

Oakhurst Baptist Church, 222 East Lake Drive, Decatur, GA. 30317. 378-7840. Open year round. 11 men.

Phyllis Wheatley YWCA, 599 Mitchell St. S.W., Atlanta, GA. 30314. 688-8792. Open year round. 35 women and children.

Saint Anthony's Catholic Church, 928 Gordon St. S.W., Atlanta, GA. 30310. 758-8861. Open Nov. 15-March 31. 35 men.

Saint Bartholomew's Episcopal Church, 1790 LaVista Road N.E., Atlanta, GA. 30329. 634-3336. Open Oct. 15-Aug. 15. 5 families.

Saint Mark United Methodist Church, 781 Peachtree St. N.E., Atlanta, GA. 30308. 873-2636. Open Nov. 1-March 31. 5 families (women and children).

Salvation Army Lodge, 400 Luckie St. N.W., Atlanta, GA. 30313. 688-2884. Open year round. 160 men, women and children.

Sanctuary Family Shelter, 1560 Memorial Drive S.E., Atlanta, GA. 30317. 378-2990, 522-5087. Open year round. 5 families.

Shearith Israel, 1180 University Drive, Atlanta, GA. 30306. 873-1743. (Shelter 873-3147.) Open Nov. 17-March 15. 12 women.

SNORE (Safe Night of Rest), 14 Waddell St., Marietta, GA. 30060. 427-9862. (Shelter 426-7667.) Open year round. 20 men and women.

The Temple, 1589 Peachtree St. N.E., Atlanta, GA. 30367. 873-1731. Open Nov. 1-March 31. 9 couples (no children).

Trinity United Methodist Church, 265 Washington St. S.W., Atlanta, GA. 30303. 659-6236. Open Nov. 1-March 31. 30 men.

United Baptist Church, 1332 Stewart Ave. S.W., Atlanta, GA. 30310. 752-5432. Open year round. 75 women and children.

West Hunter Street Baptist Church, 1040 Gordon St. S.W., Atlanta, GA. 30310. 758-1145. Open Nov. 1-April 1. 225 men.

Day Shelters

Atlanta Children's Shelter, 577 Peachtree St., Atlanta, GA. 30308. 892-7242. Open year round. 30 children.

Atlanta Day Shelter for Women, 139 Renaissance Parkway, Atlanta, GA. 30308. 876-3132. Open year round. 75 women and children.

Downtown Day Labor Service Center, 20 Coca-Cola Place, Atlanta, GA. 658-7408. Open year round. 50 men and women. Job referral and counseling.

Operation "Hope," United Seventh Day Adventist Church, 2365 Candler Road, Decatur, GA. 30032. 284-6908. Open year round. 10 men, women and children.

Samaritan House, 419 Peachtree St. N.E. (Next to Saint Luke's), Atlanta, GA. 30365. 876-3560. Open year round. 150 men and women.

Other Facilities

The Open Door Community, 910 Ponce de Leon Ave. N.E., Atlanta, GA. 30306. 874-9652. Open year round. 16 permanent residents. Daily soup kitchen. Showers. Clothing. Food care. Eye exams.

St. Luke's Health Care Clinic, 435 Peachtree St. N.E., Atlanta, GA. 30308. 873-5427. Open year round.

Mercy Mobile Hospital Project, St. Joseph's Hospital, 5665 Peachtree St., Dunwoody, GA. 30342. 851-7368. Visits shelters on schedule.

Health Clinic at Downtown Day Labor Center, 20 Coca-Cola Place, Atlanta, GA. 658-7408. By appointment.

Samaritans for Homeless Teens., 737 Woodland Ave., Atlanta, GA. 30316. 659-9403. Open year round. Referral and services for teenagers in shelters.